How to Pray the
ROSARY

Fr. Donald H. Calloway, MIC

MARIAN PRESS
STOCKBRIDGE · MA 01263

Available from:
Marian Helpers Center
Stockbridge, MA 01263

Prayerline: 1-800-804-3823
Orderline: 1-800-462-7426
Websites: fathercalloway.com
marian.org

Imprimi Potest:
Very Rev. Kazimierz Chwalek, MIC
Provincial Superior
The Blessed Virgin Mary, Mother of Mercy Province
May 31, 2016

Nihil Obstat:
Dr. Robert A. Stackpole, STD
Censor Deputatus
May 31, 2016

ISBN: 978-1-59614-397-5

Cover image: The shield insignia is a modified version of a design created by Fr. Richard Heilman for the Holy League organization. With the permission of Fr. Heilman, Fr. Calloway commissioned Jordan Barry of JB Guardian Graphics, LLC, to modify the shield insignia for *Champions of the Rosary.*
www.JBGuardianGraphics.com

Printed in the United States of America

Blessed be the Lord my rock,
who trains my hands for war, and my
fingers for battle.

~ Psalm 144:1

Though we live in the world we are not carrying on a worldly war, for the weapons of our warfare are not worldly but have divine power to destroy strongholds.

~ 2 Corinthians 10:3-4

Queen of the Rosary and St. Dominic by Vivian Imbruglia. (2016). Commissioned by Fr. Donald H. Calloway, MIC. www.sacredimageicons.com

How to Pray the Rosary

St. Dominic: Champion of the Holy Rosary by Nellie Edwards.
(2016). Commissioned by Fr. Donald H. Calloway, MIC.
www.PaintedFaith.net

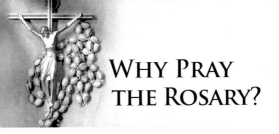

WHY PRAY THE ROSARY?

Why pray the rosary? The short answer: *It takes a sword to slay a dragon.* Dear reader, there is a serpent dragon with seven vicious heads who seeks to destroy you (see Rev 12:3). A dragon with one head is threatening enough, but a dragon with seven heads requires a heavenly weapon — the heavenly Queen's weapon. Mary will give you this weapon if you ask for it. Remember the words of Pope Leo XIII:

> The Mother of God, the Virgin most powerful, who in times past co-operated in charity that the faithful might be born in the Church, is now the intermediary, the Mediatrix of our salvation. May she shatter and strike off the multiple heads of the wicked hydra.[1]

There are, of course, many reasons why you should pray the rosary. It would be impossible to list them all. The four most important reasons are listed and explained in the pages that follow.

1
The rosary conquers the evil one

We live in a fallen world where fallen angels (demons) seek to destroy us. Such evil can only be overcome by having a greater weapon than the enemy possesses. Jesus Christ, having bound the dragon, has entrusted to his Church the weapons that enable his followers to be victorious over the evil one. These weapons are the Sacraments and the teachings of the one, holy, catholic, and apostolic Church. It is these mysteries and truths that are encapsulated in the weapon of the rosary.

The rosary is a spiritual sword made by the Divine Craftsman. Popes and saints have repeatedly emphasized this reality. Pope Leo XIII stated very clearly:

The origin of this form of prayer [the rosary] is divine rather than human.[2]

The genius of this spiritual sword is that it is easily memorized and can be prayed anywhere, anytime, and in almost all circumstances. It encapsulates the life-giving wonders of the Sacraments and the teachings of the Church, and brings them into your home and into every aspect of your life. The rosary is mobile, portable, and greatly feared by the enemy. Saint Louis de Montfort once said:

> The devils have an overwhelming fear of the rosary. Saint Bernard says that the Angelic Salutation puts them to flight and makes all hell tremble.[3]

To pray the rosary is to pray the Word of God. What better devotional prayers could ever be said than the Our Father and the Hail Mary? The words of the Our Father came from the lips of Jesus Christ himself. The words of the Angelic Salutation were uttered on God's behalf by a holy angel (St. Gabriel).

God has providentially arranged for the majority of the prayers recited in the rosary to be directed to Mary, because it is through her that the world received the instrument of our salvation, the flesh of the God-Man. Through Mary's cooperation with God, the sacred Flesh and holy mysteries of the God-Man were entrusted to the Church. Through Mary, the God-Man has conquered the darkness and vanquished the evil one forever. This mystery of salvation continues to be worked out in every generation until the end of time. It is especially through the sacred mysteries of the rosary-sword that Jesus continues to win victories over evil through his Mystical Body. Jesus himself said:

> Do not think that I have come to bring peace on earth; I have not come to bring peace, but a sword (Mt 10:34).

The rosary will make you an armed soldier, a sword-wielding knight on the battlefield of life. A rosary a day keeps the devil away!

2
The rosary preaches Jesus Christ and brings peace

The rosary is an evangelical tool that brings the light of Christ into all situations. It has the power to bring about world peace because the mysteries focus on the Truth, that is, on Jesus Christ. The original purpose of the rosary, as revealed to St. Dominic by Our Lady, was to combat heresy (false teachings). This clarification of truth was not just meant for the 13th century, but for all time, since Jesus is the same yesterday, today, and forever (see Heb 13:8). For this reason, Pope Leo XIII rightly stated:

> Our need of divine help is as great today as when the great Dominic introduced the use of the rosary of Mary as a balm for the wounds of his contemporaries.[4]

In subsequent apparitions of Our Lady, such as at Fatima, Mary reiterated that the rosary should be prayed every day in order to help people return to Jesus Christ and have peace. She even noted that the rosary has the power to stop wars. In light of that, it becomes plain that praying the rosary benefits individuals, families, and the entire world. Popes and saints have incessantly taught this reality. Pope Leo XIII emphasized the following in this regard:

> The rosary, if devoutly used, is bound to benefit not only the individual but society at large.[5]

The rosary was born in an age of chivalry. The world is once again in need of knights who are willing to fight for truth and peace. Only truth will bring about world peace. Today's knight must use this spiritual weapon to win people back to the light of the Gospel. The ability of the rosary to change hearts and bring about the reign of Christ has been proven throughout history by causing countless miracles and victories. It has saved marriages, helped turn men into saints, overcome Islam, overthrown dictators, and is one of the most richly indulgenced prayers of the Church. It even has the ability to free souls from purgatory with its indulgences. The forces of darkness in the world today threaten the very foundations of human civilization, but they are no match for the power of the rosary. Historically, the rosary has been proven to overcome all falsehoods. A rosary crusade and a new Holy League are very much needed today to bring the light and peace of Christ back into souls.

3
The rosary teaches virtue

No one ever becomes holy without acquiring virtue. All the virtues that lead to sanctity are exemplified in the lives of Jesus Christ and his Immaculate Mother. The rosary-sword is *the* sacramental that disposes souls to sanctifying grace. It is a proven fact that the rosary draws hearts closer to the Sacraments and the teachings of the Church. By its very nature, the rosary leads a person into a more fervent participation in the life of the

Church, especially faithful attendance at Holy Mass and the frequent reception of the Sacrament of Reconciliation (Confession).

In the acquisition of virtue, not only do we have fallen angels and a sinful world to overcome, but we also have the daily struggle to conquer our sinful inclinations and conform our lives to the pattern of all virtue found in Jesus and Mary. Just as children learn how to behave by looking at their parents and imitating them, so the Christian learns to become like Jesus and Mary by meditating on their virtues. The rosary is a tool to prayerfully bring those virtues to mind. Unlike the many New Age practices in the world today that are self-centered and anti-Christian, the rosary offers a form of meditation that leads the soul to true freedom, which can only be found in Jesus Christ. For this reason, the rosary is therapeutic and healing. It helps a person to conquer vice, stop sinning, and acquire virtue. The rosary is heavenly medicine, an antidote that draws the poison of sin and vice out of our hearts.

Perseverance in praying the rosary has proven to be a tremendous means of helping a person avoid sin and remain in a state of grace. Saint Louis de Montfort once wrote:

> It was because Our Lady wanted to help us in the great task of working out our salvation that she ordered St. Dominic to teach the faithful to meditate upon the sacred mysteries of the life of Jesus Christ. She did this, not only that they might adore and glorify him, but chiefly that they might pattern their lives and actions upon his virtues.[6]

This is one of the many reasons why the rosary is the favored prayer of the saints. The rosary will help you become holy.

4

The rosary is an expression of our love for Jesus and Mary

All people who are in love never tire of telling each other, "I love you." This is also true for parents and their children. Telling someone you love them can have the appearance of a merely repetitious statement, since the same words are repeated over and over again, but everyone knows that telling someone they are loved is never routine or boring. Every time the phrase is uttered, it is new and fresh. The Venerable Fulton Sheen understood this and shared the following insight:

> When we say the rosary — we are saying to God, the Trinity, to the Incarnate Savior, to the Blessed Mother: "I love you, I love you, I love you."[7]

By praying the rosary, we express our gratitude to Jesus and Mary by "calling to mind" the tremendous sacrificial love that they have for us. This act moves the

Sacred Heart of Jesus and the Immaculate Heart of Mary to pour out countless graces upon us. Expressions of love from us are reciprocated by gifts of love from heaven.

Saints and popes have often noted in their writings that no one is capable of loving Mary more than Jesus. Therefore, Jesus is not offended when we pray the rosary. On the contrary, he himself takes great delight in the praying of the rosary by his disciples because to pray the rosary is to lay spiritual roses at the feet of his mother. This practice would never offend him. All children would do well to bring flowers to their mother as an expression of love. Would Jesus not inspire others to perform the same loving acts toward his mother that he himself does? After all, he shared the gift of his mother with all of his disciples as he was hanging from the Cross. Thus, when we pray the rosary, we, too, are able to lay lovely garlands of roses at the feet of our beautiful mother. This practice brings joy to the heart of our spiritual mother and greatly pleases the heart of our Savior.

When we pray the rosary, we show that we are faithful to the Word of God, which explicitly states that *all* generations are to call Mary blessed (see Lk 1:48). As Bl. James Alberione succinctly put it:

> The rosary is the easiest way to honor God and the Blessed Virgin. It is the surest way to triumph over spiritual enemies, the most suitable way to progress in virtue and sanctity.[8]

How to Pray the Rosary

The rosary is very easy to pray. It can be prayed on your own or with others. The most important thing to remember about praying the rosary is that it is a blending of vocal and mental (meditative) prayer. Saint Louis de Montfort once remarked:

> I know of no better way of establishing the kingdom of God than to unite vocal and mental prayer by saying the rosary.[1]

The combination of vocal and mental prayer makes the rosary a prayer of the body and also a prayer of the soul. Having stated this, it is important to remember that if you pray the rosary by yourself, you do not need to vocalize the prayers with your lips.

When praying the rosary, it is better to pray it on one's knees, since this is the most pious position for prayer. Not everyone is able to kneel due to health issues and/or age, and so it is perfectly acceptable to pray the rosary while sitting, walking, exercising, driving, etc. For those who are unfamiliar with the structure of the rosary, a diagram will be presented at the end of this section that includes the prayers associated with the rosary, how it is to be prayed, and a list of the 20 mysteries, as well as which mysteries are prayed on different days of the week. What follows below is a brief description of the vocal and meditative aspects of the rosary.

1
Vocal Prayer

When the rosary is prayed on your own, it should take at least 15 to 20 minutes. It is possible to spend more than 20 minutes praying the rosary and taking more time to meditate on the mysteries. If a person prays the rosary in less than

15 minutes, they are praying it too fast because there really is no way a person can devoutly meditate on the mysteries and say the prayers reverently in less time than that. If a person prays the rosary with other people, the normal amount of time that should be allotted is 20 minutes — no less. There are several dangers to avoid when praying the rosary in a group, including praying the rosary too fast, too slow, too loudly, or emphasizing certain words over others.

Saint Louis de Montfort had the following to say about those who pray the rosary too fast:

> It is really pathetic to see how most people say the holy rosary — they say it astonishingly fast and mumble so that the words are not properly pronounced at all. We could not possibly expect anyone, even the most unimportant person, to think that a slipshod address of this kind was a compliment and yet we expect Jesus and Mary to be pleased with it![2]

These are strong words, but he is absolutely correct. If you have ever tried to pray the rosary with someone who speeds through it, it becomes an endurance test, a burden, and a barely-tolerated act of piety for everyone else. Such a rosary is hardly a meditative prayer at all. As the famous Dominican rosary priest Fr. Gabriel Harty once noted:

> *Speed Kills* is what the road sign shouts. So too with the highway of the rosary. Speed destroys its rhythm and kills the spirit, and the principal victim is the holy name of Jesus.[3]

In other words, when the rosary is prayed in common, everyone should pray it at the same pace, a pace that is not hurried or rushed. Saint Anthony Mary Claret used to instruct his seminarians that when they prayed the rosary, they were to remember that their words were addressed to the King of Kings and the Queen of Heaven and earth. In this regard, he noted the following:

The rosary should not be prayed hastily, but slowly and with devotion, pronouncing all of the words well, and not starting one part until the other has finished.[4]

Those who pray the rosary in common should also remember that the rosary is not to be prayed too slowly, either. If you have ever prayed the rosary with someone who drags out every word, their voice becomes a distraction and makes the others in attendance feel like they are pushing a heavy train through molasses. When the rosary is prayed too slowly, the other participants cannot meditate because their focus is being drawn to the unnatural pace of the slow person. Forcing others to pray the rosary at that pace is neither charitable nor prayerful for the others in the group.

The rosary is being prayed perfectly when all the members pray it at the same natural and prayerful pace. This gives the rosary a beautiful rhythm, flow, and harmonious timing that match normal breathing patterns. On the other hand, if one member prays too loudly, allowing his voice and pace to dominate the others, everyone automatically begins to focus on his voice and is no longer able to meditate; the vocal aspect becomes a distraction for all the other members. Similarly, if a person places an emphasis on one particular word of the Hail Mary prayer, it breaks the flow and rhythm of the group's timing. All of the above aspects should be taken seriously, because a group's failure to pray the rosary well and harmoniously is often the reason why many people do not join in praying the rosary before or after Mass. Very few people are interested in praying a rosary that is chaotic and a verbal wrestling match. If you desire to hear a perfectly timed and well-prayed communal rosary, visit any chapel of the Missionaries of Charity and listen to how they pray the rosary in common.

2
Meditative Prayer

It is true that most people become easily distracted when praying the rosary. Almost everyone will find their mind wandering away from the mysteries at least once. Even saints struggled with this. God is well aware that we are neither angels nor robots, and do not have the ability to ponder one thing for long periods of time without other things coming to mind. Saint Thérèse of Lisieux expressed her struggles this way:

> I feel that I say the rosary so poorly! I make a concentrated effort to meditate on the mysteries of the rosary, but I am unable to focus my concentration. For a long time I was disconsolate about my lack of devotion, which astonished me since I so much loved the Blessed Virgin that it ought to have been easy for me to recite the prayers in her honor that so much pleased her. But now I am less sad, for I think that the Queen of heaven, who is also my Mother, ought to see my good intentions and that she is pleased with them.[5]

Everyone who prays the rosary is going to lose their concentration and find their mind wandering from time to time. Do not let this discourage you. Praying the rosary is an act of the will because it is an act of love. Feelings will come and go. True love perseveres through difficulties, distractions, and no sensible consolation. When distractions come, simply re-focus your mind on the mystery at hand. This may occur many times throughout the rosary, but it is very pleasing to Jesus and Mary when a person turns their mind and heart back to the mysteries. Saint Louis de Montfort noted the following in this regard:

> Even if you have to fight distractions all through your whole rosary, be sure to fight well, arms in hand: that is to say, do not stop saying your rosary even if it is hard to say and you have absolutely no sensible devotion. It is a terrible battle, I know, but one that is profitable to the faithful soul.[6]

A person will learn many virtues by perseverance in praying the rosary and, over time, will acquire the ability to become less distracted and more focused on the mysteries. The Servant of God Dolindo Ruotolo offers these consoling and encouraging words for those who struggle in this area:

> To know how to pray is a gift of God. It is part of the gift of piety, a gift of the Holy Spirit. With diligent practice every day, it is possible to succeed in reciting the holy rosary worthily.[7]

Perseverance makes a champion!

Praying the Rosary

1. Make the Sign of the Cross and say the "Apostles' Creed."

2. Say the "Our Father."

3. Say three "Hail Marys."

4. Say the "Glory be to the Father."

5. Announce the First Mystery; then say the "Our Father."

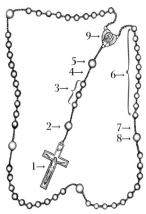

6. Say 10 "Hail Marys" while meditating on the Mystery.

7. Say the "Glory be to the Father." After each decade, say the following prayer requested by the Blessed Virgin Mary at Fatima: "O my Jesus, forgive us our sins, save us from the fires of hell, lead all souls to Heaven, especially those in most need of Thy mercy."

8. Announce the Second Mystery: then say the "Our Father." Repeat 6 and 7 and continue with the Third, Fourth, and Fifth Mysteries in the same manner.

9. Say the "Hail, Holy Queen" and the concluding prayer on the medal after the five decades are completed.

As a general rule, depending on the liturgical season, the various Mysteries of the rosary are prayed on the following days of the week:

Sunday: Glorious Mysteries
Monday: Joyful Mysteries
Tuesday: Sorrowful Mysteries
Wednesday: Glorious Mysteries
Thursday: Luminous Mysteries
Friday: Sorrowful Mysteries
Saturday: Joyful Mysteries

Prayers of the Rosary

THE SIGN OF THE CROSS

In the name of the Father, and of the Son, and of the Holy Spirit. Amen.

THE APOSTLES' CREED

I believe in God, the Father almighty, Creator of heaven and earth, and in Jesus Christ, his only Son, our Lord, who was conceived by the Holy Spirit, born of the Virgin Mary, suffered under Pontius Pilate, was crucified, died, and was buried; he descended into hell; on the third day he rose again from the dead; he ascended into heaven, and is seated at the right hand of God the Father almighty; from there he will come to judge the living and the dead. I believe in the Holy Spirit, the holy catholic Church, the communion of saints, the forgiveness of sins, the resurrection of the body, and life everlasting. Amen.

The wording of the Apostles' Creed conforms with the Roman Missal.

OUR FATHER

Our Father, who art in heaven; hallowed be Thy name; Thy kingdom come; Thy will be done on earth as it is in heaven. Give us this day our daily bread; and forgive us our trespasses as we forgive those who trespass against us, and lead us not into temptation; but deliver us from evil. Amen.

HAIL MARY

Hail Mary, full of grace. The Lord is with thee. Blessed art thou among women, and blessed is the fruit of thy womb, Jesus. Holy Mary, Mother of God, pray for us sinners, now and at the hour of our death. Amen.

GLORY BE TO THE FATHER

Glory be to the Father, and to the Son, and to the Holy Spirit. As it was in the beginning, is now, and ever shall be, world without end. Amen.

FATIMA PRAYER

O my Jesus, forgive us our sins, save us from the fires of hell. Lead all souls to Heaven, especially those most in need of Thy mercy.

HAIL, HOLY QUEEN

Hail, Holy Queen, Mother of Mercy, our life, our sweetness, and our hope, to thee do we cry, poor banished children of Eve; to thee do we send up our sighs, mourning and weeping in this valley of tears; turn, then, most gracious Advocate, thine eyes of mercy towards us, and after this, our exile, show unto us the blessed fruit of thy womb, Jesus. O clement, O loving, O sweet Virgin Mary!

Pray for us, O holy Mother of God, that we may be made worthy of the promises of Christ.

CONCLUDING PRAYER

O God, whose only begotten Son, by His life, death, and resurrection, has purchased for us the rewards of eternal life, grant, we beseech Thee, that by meditating on these mysteries of the most holy Rosary of the Blessed Virgin Mary, we may imitate what they contain and obtain what they promise, through the same Christ our Lord. Amen.

Mysteries of the Rosary

JOYFUL MYSTERIES

FIRST JOYFUL MYSTERY
THE ANNUNCIATION

And when the angel had come to her, he said, "Hail, full of grace, the Lord is with you" (Lk 1:28).

One Our Father, 10 Hail Marys, One Glory Be, etc.

FRUIT OF THE MYSTERY: *HUMILITY*

SECOND JOYFUL MYSTERY
THE VISITATION

Elizabeth, filled with the holy Spirit, cried out in a loud voice and said, "Most blessed are you among women, and blessed is the fruit of your womb" (Lk 1:41-42).

One Our Father, 10 Hail Marys, One Glory Be, etc.

FRUIT OF THE MYSTERY: *LOVE OF NEIGHBOR*

THIRD JOYFUL MYSTERY
THE BIRTH OF JESUS

She gave birth to her first-born Son. She wrapped Him in swaddling clothes and laid Him in a manger, because there was no room for them in the inn (Lk 2:7).

One Our Father, 10 Hail Marys, One Glory Be, etc.

FRUIT OF THE MYSTERY: *POVERTY IN SPIRIT*

FOURTH JOYFUL MYSTERY
THE PRESENTATION

When the days were completed for their purification according to the law of Moses, they took Him up to Jerusalem to present Him to the Lord, just as it is written in the law of the Lord, "Every male that opens the womb shall be consecrated to the Lord" (Lk 2:22-23).

One Our Father, 10 Hail Marys, One Glory Be, etc.

FRUIT OF THE MYSTERY: *OBEDIENCE*

FIFTH JOYFUL MYSTERY
FINDING THE CHILD JESUS IN THE TEMPLE

After three days they found Him in the temple, sitting in the midst of the teachers, listening to them and asking them questions (Lk 2:46).

One Our Father, 10 Hail Marys, One Glory Be, etc.

FRUIT OF THE MYSTERY: *JOY IN FINDING JESUS*

LUMINOUS MYSTERIES

FIRST LUMINOUS MYSTERY
BAPTISM OF JESUS

After Jesus was baptized, … the heavens were opened, and he saw the Spirit of God descending like a dove [and] coming upon Him. And a voice came from the heavens, saying, "This is My beloved Son, with whom I am well pleased" (Mt 3:16-17).

One Our Father, 10 Hail Marys, One Glory Be, etc.

FRUIT OF THE MYSTERY: *OPENNESS TO THE HOLY SPIRIT*

SECOND LUMINOUS MYSTERY
WEDDING AT CANA

His mother said to the servers, "Do whatever He tells you." … Jesus told them, "Fill the jars with water." So they filled them to the brim (Jn 2:5-7).

One Our Father, 10 Hail Marys, One Glory Be, etc.

FRUIT OF THE MYSTERY: *TO JESUS THROUGH MARY*

THIRD LUMINOUS MYSTERY
PROCLAIMING THE KINGDOM

"As you go, make this proclamation: 'The kingdom of heaven is at hand.' Cure the sick, raise the dead, cleanse lepers, drive out demons. Without cost you have received; without cost you are to give" (Mt 10:7-8).

One Our Father, 10 Hail Marys, One Glory Be, etc.

FRUIT OF THE MYSTERY: *REPENTANCE AND TRUST IN GOD*

FOURTH LUMINOUS MYSTERY

TRANSFIGURATION

While He was praying His face changed in appearance and His clothing became dazzling white. Then from the cloud came a voice that said, "This is My chosen Son; listen to Him" (Lk 9:29, 35).

One Our Father, 10 Hail Marys, One Glory Be, etc.

FRUIT OF THE MYSTERY: *DESIRE FOR HOLINESS*

FIFTH LUMINOUS MYSTERY

INSTITUTION OF THE EUCHARIST

Then He took the bread, said the blessing, broke it, and gave it to them, saying, "This is My body, which will be given for you ..." And likewise the cup after they had eaten, saying, "This cup is the new covenant in My blood" (Lk 22:19-20).

One Our Father, 10 Hail Marys, One Glory Be, etc.

FRUIT OF THE MYSTERY: *ADORATION*

SORROWFUL MYSTERIES

FIRST SORROWFUL MYSTERY

THE AGONY IN THE GARDEN

He was in such agony and He prayed so fervently that His sweat became like drops of blood falling on the ground. When He rose from prayer and returned to His disciples, He found them sleeping from grief (Lk 22:44-45).

One Our Father, 10 Hail Marys, One Glory Be, etc.

FRUIT OF THE MYSTERY:
SORROW FOR SIN

SECOND SORROWFUL MYSTERY

THE SCOURGING AT THE PILLAR

Then Pilate took Jesus and had Him scourged (Jn 19:1).

One Our Father, 10 Hail Marys, One Glory Be, etc.

FRUIT OF THE MYSTERY:
PURITY

THIRD SORROWFUL MYSTERY

CROWNING WITH THORNS

They stripped off His clothes and threw a scarlet military cloak about Him. Weaving a crown out of thorns, they placed it on His head, and a reed in His right hand (Mt 27:28-29).

One Our Father, 10 Hail Marys, One Glory Be, etc.

FRUIT OF THE MYSTERY: *COURAGE*

FOURTH SORROWFUL MYSTERY

CARRYING OF THE CROSS

And carrying the cross Himself, He went out to what is called the Place of the Skull, in Hebrew, Golgotha (Jn 19:17).

One Our Father, 10 Hail Marys, One Glory Be, etc.

FRUIT OF THE MYSTERY: *PATIENCE*

FIFTH SORROWFUL MYSTERY
THE CRUCIFIXION

Jesus cried out in a loud voice, "Father, into Your hands I commend My spirit"; and when He had said this He breathed His last (Lk 23:46).

One Our Father, 10 Hail Marys, One Glory Be, etc.

FRUIT OF THE MYSTERY: *PERSEVERANCE*

GLORIOUS MYSTERIES

FIRST GLORIOUS MYSTERY
THE RESURRECTION

"Do not be amazed! You seek Jesus of Nazareth, the crucified. He has been raised; He is not here. Behold the place where they laid Him" (Mk 16:6).

One Our Father, 10 Hail Marys, One Glory Be, etc.

FRUIT OF THE MYSTERY: *FAITH*

SECOND GLORIOUS MYSTERY

THE ASCENSION

So then the Lord Jesus, after He spoke to them, was taken up into heaven and took His seat at the right hand of God (Mk 16:19).

One Our Father, 10 Hail Marys, One Glory Be, etc.

FRUIT OF THE MYSTERY: *HOPE*

THIRD GLORIOUS MYSTERY

DESCENT OF THE HOLY SPIRIT

And they were all filled with the Holy Spirit and began to speak in different tongues, as the Spirit enabled them to proclaim (Acts 2:4).

One Our Father, 10 Hail Marys, One Glory Be, etc.

FRUIT OF THE MYSTERY: *LOVE OF GOD*

FOURTH GLORIOUS MYSTERY

THE ASSUMPTION

"You are the glory of Jerusalem! ... You are the great boast of our nation! ... You have done good things for Israel, and God is pleased with them. May the Almighty Lord bless you forever!" (Jud 15:9-10).

One Our Father, 10 Hail Marys, One Glory Be, etc.

FRUIT OF THE MYSTERY:
GRACE OF A HAPPY DEATH

FIFTH GLORIOUS MYSTERY

THE CORONATION

A great sign appeared in the sky, a woman clothed with the sun, with the moon under her feet, and on her head a crown of twelve stars (Rev 12:1).

One Our Father, 10 Hail Marys, One Glory Be, etc.

FRUIT OF THE MYSTERY:
TRUST IN MARY'S INTERCESSION

Image of Mary taken from *The 26 Champions of the Rosary* by Maria Madonna Bouza Urbina. (2016). Commissioned by Fr. Donald H. Calloway, MIC. www.fathercalloway.com

HOW TO BECOME A CHAMPION OF THE ROSARY

To be a champion of the rosary, it is not necessary to write books on the rosary or give conferences about it. All that is needed is a heart docile to the Holy Spirit and a desire to make the rosary more known. Here are three simple methods that allow anyone to become a champion of the rosary:

1
Pray the rosary

During a papal visit to the Shrine of Our Lady of the Rosary of Pompeii, Pope Benedict XVI provided the following understanding of what is required in order to become a champion of the rosary. He stated:

To be apostles of the rosary it is necessary to experience personally the beauty and depth of this prayer which is simple and accessible to everyone. It is first of all necessary to let the Blessed Virgin Mary take one by the hand to contemplate the Face of Christ: a joyful, luminous, sorrowful and glorious face.[1]

In other words, a person cannot give what a person does not have. Thus, it is first necessary for a person to pray the rosary himself; only then can he truly and effectively became an apostle and champion of the rosary. It is from personal experience and a love for the rosary that champions and apostles of the rosary are born.

In becoming a champion of the rosary, it is important to remember that praying the rosary is not about experiencing good feelings. Many times, as in any relationship, pleasant feelings come and go. What determines one's faithfulness in any relationship is perseverance through the difficult and dry times. Champions of the rosary are made when a soul perseveres in praying the rosary, no matter what. Love endures dryness and is consistent in all seasons of life, whether those seasons are joyful, luminous, sorrowful, or glorious. Saint Louis de Montfort knew this and noted the following about persevering in praying the rosary:

> Even if you suffer from dryness of soul, boredom and interior discouragement, never give up even the least little bit of your rosary. On the contrary, like a real champion of Jesus and Mary, you should say your Our Fathers and Hail Marys quite drily if you have to, without seeing, hearing or feeling any consolation whatsoever, and concentrating as best you can on the mysteries.[2]

True champions of the rosary never give up!

2

Encourage others to pray the rosary

It is only natural that after having experienced the power of the rosary to conquer evil, you would desire to hand on the great spiritual sword to another. Like St. Louis de Montfort, we should want to tell the whole world about the great secret of the rosary so that they, too, might tap into its power. A champion of the rosary will have at his disposal a plethora of means to spread the devotion of the rosary to others, such as praying for others to be lit on fire with the same burning love for Our Lady and her rosary as the great champions of the rosary, as well as sharing rosary beads and giving away good books on the rosary to family members, friends, godchildren, fellow parishioners, and co-workers. Many saints followed this last method of spreading the rosary through sharing good books. Blessed James Alberione had these encouraging words to say about how to promote the rosary:

Make Mary known and loved by others. Invite all to go to Mary. Where Mary enters, Jesus follows. Through Mary to Jesus. Foster the recitation of the rosary in every family. The fruits will be numberless, and we will be able to count them only in heaven. Diffuse books and pamphlets on the rosary; speak of this devotion; exhort its recitation on all good occasions which present themselves. Also give the example: the rosary witnesses to itself. One who sees the rosary beads in the hands of another will feel the desire to do the same, will receive a first grace, that is, will at least conceive a good thought.[3]

As a concrete way of passing on the knowledge of the rosary, it is recommended that a champion of the rosary seek to give away copies of the following three books on the rosary:

– *The Secret of the Rosary* by St. Louis de Montfort
– *Champions of the Rosary: The History and Heroes of a Spiritual Weapon* by Fr. Donald Calloway, MIC

— *Rosary Gems: Daily Wisdom on the Holy Rosary* by Fr. Donald Calloway, MIC

In addition to evangelizing others by giving them one of the three books above, if your parish does not have a rosary prayer group, try to start one. Always be sure to get the permission of the pastor of the parish first, however. Most times, pastors are very favorable to such practices, and will have no problem with people praying the rosary either before or after Mass. Most priests find that this practice fosters a greater sense of devotion in the hearts and souls of their parishioners and leads to a greater participation in the life of the Church.

Other ways to encourage the faithful to pray the rosary, as Bl. Alberione and so many other saints have noted, is to begin to pray it as a family and as spouses. It is also a highly praiseworthy practice for a family to initiate a weekly rosary prayer group in their home and invite other families and parishioners over to pray the rosary. Once this practice catches on, the families and parishioners can begin to alternate homes so that a community of faith is formed and relationships are built. This practice is certain to bring about devout Catholic communities and help build holy families and devout parishes. Whatever way you seek to encourage others to pray the rosary, remember the words of St. Louis de Montfort:

> Our Lady blesses not only those who preach her rosary, but she highly rewards all those who get others to say it by their example.[4]

3
Join an official organization that promotes the rosary

Joining an official organization that promotes the rosary is an extraordinary way to champion the rosary and share in the spiritual benefits of the organization. Many of these organizations function as spiritual benefit societies and offer their members many blessings. Organizations such as the Association of Marian Helpers, the Thirteenth of the Month Club, the Legion of Mary, the Schoenstatt Rosary Campaign, the Militia Immaculatae, the World Apostolate of Fatima, and Holy Cross Family Ministries are some of the great organizations that you can join to help spread the rosary.

Two rosary organizations that I particularly recommend are the Thirteenth of the Month Club and the Confraternity of the Rosary. The Thirteenth of the Month Club, based out of Stockbridge, Massachusetts, is operated by the Marian Fathers of the Immaculate Conception, the religious congregation to which I belong. The Marian Fathers operate the National Shrine of The Divine Mercy in Stockbridge and are a zealous group of men promoting devotion to Our Lady (especially as the Immaculate Conception), the Divine Mercy message and devotion, Marian consecration, and the rosary. As the spiritual director for the Thirteenth of the Month Club, I can assure you that it is a very worthwhile group to join, a great way to champion the rosary, and a true means of offering support for a very orthodox Marian religious community. I strongly encourage you to find out more about the Thirteenth of the Month Club and become a member:

Thirteenth of the Month Club
Eden Hill
Stockbridge, MA 01263
1-800-462-7426
www.marian.org/13th

The other rosary organization that I most highly recommend is the Confraternity of the Rosary. This is the worldwide organization that was founded by St. Dominic, renewed by Bl. Alan de la Roche, and has been promoted by many popes. In the United States, contact the Confraternity at either of the following two locations:

Confraternity of the Rosary
PO Box 3617
Portland, OR 97208
1-503-236-8393
www.rosary-center.org

Confraternity of the Rosary
280 North Grant Ave.
Columbus, OH 43215
1-614-240-5929
www.rosaryconfraternity.org

In addition to the above rosary organizations, I also highly recommend that all Catholic men join the Holy League movement, founded in Wisconsin in 2014. This organization has its spiritual headquarters at the Shrine of Our Lady of Guadalupe in La Crosse, Wisconsin; Cardinal Raymond Burke is its spiritual head. The Holy League is a parish-based network of men dedicated to fighting against the evils of our day by means of a monthly Eucharistic Holy Hour, which includes making available the Sacrament of Confession and praying the rosary. It is done in an effort to help Catholic men remain strong in the power of grace.

Holy League
PO Box 1266
La Crosse, WI 54602
www.holyleague.com

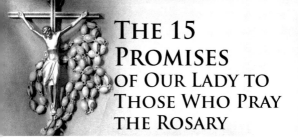

THE 15 PROMISES OF OUR LADY TO THOSE WHO PRAY THE ROSARY

1. To all those who shall recite my rosary devoutly, I promise my special protection and very great graces.

2. Those who shall persevere in the recitation of my rosary shall receive signal graces.

3. The rosary shall be a very powerful armor against hell; it will destroy vice, deliver from sin, and dispel heresy.

4. The rosary will make virtue and good works flourish, and will obtain for souls the most abundant divine mercies; it will draw the hearts of men from the love of the world to the love of God, and will lift them to the desire of eternal things. How many souls shall sanctify themselves by this means!

5. Those who trust themselves to me through the rosary shall not perish.

6. Those who shall recite my rosary devoutly, meditating on its mysteries, shall not be overwhelmed by misfortune. The sinner shall be converted; the just shall grow in grace and become worthy of eternal life.

7. Those truly devoted to my rosary shall not die without the Sacraments of the Church.

8. Those who faithfully recite my rosary shall find during their life and at the hour of their death the light of God, the fullness of his graces, and shall share in the merits of the blessed.

9. I shall deliver very promptly from purgatory the souls devoted to my rosary.

10. The true children of my rosary shall enjoy great glory in heaven.

11. What you ask through my rosary, you shall obtain.

12. Those who propagate my rosary will be aided by me in all their necessities.

13. I have obtained from my Son that all the members of the Rosary Confraternity shall have as their intercessors, in life and in death, the entire celestial court.

14. Those who recite my rosary faithfully are all my beloved children, the brothers and sisters of Jesus Christ.

15. Devotion to my rosary is a great sign of predestination.

* The above list is taken from a book by the Servant of God Patrick Peyton.[1]

Madonna of the Rosary (c. 1605). Caravaggio (1571-1610).
Kunsthistorisches Museum. Vienna, Austria. Public Domain.

INDULGENCES OF THE ROSARY

People are often quite unaware of how rich the rosary is in indulgences. This is because many priests, when preaching on the rosary, hardly ever mention indulgences and give rather a flowery and popular sermon which excites admiration but scarcely teaches anything.[1]

~ St. Louis de Montfort

The words above serve as a reminder that, over the course of the centuries, there have been many indulgences given by the Church to those who pray the rosary. The Catholic Church is the storehouse of the graces of the redemption, and the Savior works through his Mystical Body to dispense many of these graces to souls in the form of pardons. These gifts are not magic, but rather graces and mercies that flow from the heart of a merciful God who loves his children. Our Heavenly Father is more than willing to indulge us with his mercy and love.

On January 1, 1967, Bl. Pope Paul VI promulgated a revision of the sacred indulgences available to the Church in an apostolic constitution titled *Indulgentiarum Doctrina*. It was published on June 29, 1968 and has since undergone several editions. On July 5, 1999, in preparation for the Jubilee celebrations for the third Christian millennium, St. John Paul II approved a revised fourth edition. Then, on October 12, 2005, the Apostolic Penitentiary in Rome approved the English translation of the text, now known in English as the *Manual of Indulgences.*

Below are the selected and pertinent *Norms* from the *Manual of Indulgences* that the reader will find helpful for understanding what an indulgence is (plenary or partial), how often one may be obtained, and what conditions must be met to gain it. Presented at the end are the specific indulgenced Grants from the *Manual of Indulgences* that the Church offers to those who pray the rosary.

NORMS

n. 1 — An indulgence is a remission before God of the temporal punishment for sins, whose guilt is forgiven, which a properly disposed member of the Christian faithful obtains under certain and clearly defined conditions through the intervention of the Church, which, as the minister of Redemption, dispenses and applies authoritatively the treasury of the expiatory works of Christ and the saints.

n. 2 — An indulgence is partial or plenary according to whether it removes either part or all of the temporal punishment due sin.

n. 3 — The faithful can obtain partial or plenary indulgences for themselves, or they can apply them to the dead [souls in purgatory] by way of suffrage. [No one gaining an indulgence may apply it to other living persons.]

n. 15 — The faithful can acquire an indulgence if they use devoutly one of the following properly blessed pious objects, namely, a crucifix or cross, rosary, scapular, or medal.

n. 17 — In order to be capable of gaining indulgences one must be baptized, not excommunicated, and in the state of grace at least at the completion of the prescribed works.

n. 18 — A plenary indulgence can be acquired only once in the course of a day; a partial indulgence can be acquired multiple times.

n. 20 — To gain a plenary indulgence, in addition to excluding all attachment to sin, even venial sin, it is necessary to perform the indulgenced work and fulfill the following three conditions: sacramental confession, Eucharistic Communion, and prayer for the intention of the Sovereign Pontiff.

- The three conditions may be fulfilled several days before or after the performance of the prescribed work; it is, however, fitting that Communion be received and the prayer for the intention of the

Holy Father be said on the same day the work is performed.

• The condition of praying for the intention of the Holy Father is fully satisfied by reciting one Our Father and one Hail Mary; nevertheless, one has the option of reciting any other prayer according to individual piety and devotion, if recited for this intention.

* Many numbers have not been presented because they are not pertinent to the topic at hand.

GRANTS

n. 17 — Prayers to the Blessed Virgin Mary

A plenary indulgence is granted to the faithful who

> • devoutly recite the Marian rosary in a church or oratory, or in a family, a religious community, or an association of the faithful, and in general when several of the faithful gather for some honest purpose;

• devoutly join in the recitation of the rosary while it is being recited by the Supreme Pontiff and broadcast live by radio or television. In other circumstances, the indulgence will be *partial*.

NB: According to the *Manual of Indulgences*, the plenary indulgence is gained when only five decades of the rosary are recited. However, the five decades must be recited without interruption.[2]

REFERENCES

Why Pray the Rosary?

[1] Pope Leo XIII, *Parta Humano Generi,* Apostolic Letter (September 8, 1901), as quoted in *The Rosary of Our Lady: Translations of the Encyclical and Apostolic Letters of Pope Leo XIII*, ed. William Raymond Lawler, OP (Paterson, NJ: St. Anthony Guild Press, 1944), 195-196.

[2] Pope Leo XIII, *Diuturni Temporis,* Encyclical (September 5, 1898), 3.

[3] St. Louis de Montfort, *The Secret of the Rosary,* 80-81.

[4] Pope Leo XIII, *Supremi Apostolatus Officio,* 7.

[5] Pope Leo XIII, *Laetitiae Sanctae,* Encyclical (September 8, 1893), 3.

[6] St. Louis de Montfort, *The Secret of the Rosary,* 56.

[7] Ven. Fulton J. Sheen, *The World's First Love: Mary, Mother of God* (San Francisco: Ignatius Press, 1996), 208.

[8] Bl. James Alberione, *Mary, Mother and Model: Feasts of Mary,* trans. Hilda Calabro, MA (Boston, MA: Daughters of St. Paul, 1958), 201.

How to Pray the Rosary

[1] St. Louis de Montfort, *God Alone: The Collected Writings of St. Louis de Montfort.* (Bay Shore, NY: Montfort Publications, 1995), 104.

[2] St. Louis de Montfort, *The Secret of the Rosary,* trans. Mary Barbour, TOP (Bay Shore, NY: Montfort Publications, 1988), 93.

[3] Gabriel Harty, OP, *Heaven Sent: My Life Through the Rosary* (Dublin, Ireland: Veritas, 2012), 153.

[4] St. Anthony Mary Claret, *El Colegial Ó Seminarista Teórica y Prácticamente Instruido: Tome I.* (Barcelona, Spain: Librería Religiosa, 1861), 278. Trans. Miss Ileana E. Salazar, MA.

[5] St. Thérèse of Lisieux, as quoted in Romanus Cessario, OP, *Perpetual Angelus: As the Saints Pray the Rosary* (Staten Island, NY: Alba House, 1995), 136.

[6] St. Louis de Montfort, *The Secret of the Rosary*, 91.

[7] Servant of God Dolindo Ruotolo, *Meditations on the Holy Rosary of Mary,* trans. Giovanna Invitti Ellis (Napoli, Italy, 2006), 37.

How to Become a Champion of the Rosary

[1] Pope Benedict XVI, *Meditation from the Pastoral Visit to Shrine of Pompeii* (October 19, 2008).

[2] St. Louis de Montfort, *The Secret of the Rosary,* trans. Mary Barbour, TOP (Bay Shore, NY: Montfort Publications, 1988), 103.

[3] Bl. James Alberione, *Lord, Teach Us to Pray* (Boston, MA: Daughters of St. Paul, 1982), 231.

[4] St. Louis de Montfort, *The Secret of the Rosary,* 28.

The 15 Promises of Our Lady To Those Who Pray the Rosary

[1] Servant of God Patrick Peyton, *The Ear of God* (Garden City, NJ: Doubleday & Company, Inc., 1951), 114-115.

Indulgences of the Rosary

[1] St. Louis de Montfort, *The Secret of the Rosary,* trans. Mary Barbour, TOP (Bay Shore, NY: Montfort Publications, 1988), 86.

[2] *Manual of Indulgences: Norms and Grants.* United States Catholic Conference of Bishops Publishing (December 1, 2006).

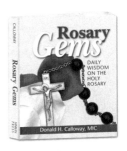

Champions of the Rosary T-Shirt

Show your love of the Rosary with this t-shirt bearing the cover image of Fr. Donald Calloway's book, *Champions of the Rosary* — the perfect gift for

those who want to spread their love for this devotion! T-shirts are black cotton/polyester blend and come in a variety of sizes.

Champions of the Rosary in Canvas Art

Commissioned by Fr. Donald Calloway, "The 26 Champions of the Rosary" image was painted by artist Maria Madonna Bouza Urbina in 2016. Now available on canvas, the image depicts the Blessed Mother holding the rosary and a sword, surrounded by 26 individuals who made the rosary central to their very being. Father Calloway tells the stories of how they lived out their love for this devotion in his book. Image size is 10" x 18".

Canvas image with Champions of the Rosary: Y69-RC10GW

Canvas image with names of 26 Champions of the Rosary: Y69-CR10GW

Call 1-800-462-7426

Father Donald Calloway, MIC, Marian vocation director, participates in a recurring feature in the Thirteenth of the Month Club newsletter.

I'm honored and delighted to do this for the club, since it's a good way for me to help people come to a better place in their relationship with Our Lady. I want to let people know that by being in the Thirteenth of the Month Club, they're part of the Marian family. They are praying for us [the Marian Fathers of the Immaculate Conception], and we are praying for them.

Thirteenth of the Month Club members are a group of special friends who help support the work of the Marian Fathers of the Immaculate Conception. On the 13th of each month, members pray the Rosary for the intentions of the Club. The Marians residing in Fatima offer a special Mass on the 13th of the month for members' intentions. All members pledge a monthly gift and receive the Club newsletter, published by the Association of Marian Helpers, Stockbridge, MA 01263.

For more information, call: 1-413-298-1382
Online: marian.org/13th
E-mail: thirteenth@marian.org

Marian Helpers

Join the
Association of Marian Helpers,
headquartered at the
National Shrine of The Divine Mercy,
and share in special blessings!

**An invitation from
Fr. Joseph, MIC, the director**

**Marian Helpers is
an Association of
Christian faithful of
the Congregation
of Marian
Fathers of the
Immaculate
Conception.**

By becoming a member, you share in
the spiritual benefits of the daily Masses,
prayers, and good works of the Marian
priests and brothers.

This is a special offer of grace given to
you by the Church through the Marians.
Please consider this opportunity to share
in these blessings, along with others
whom you would wish to join into this
spiritual communion.

**Call 1-800-462-7426
or visit marian.org**